SIU

THE SET, THEORY, MAIN-POINTS, MOTTOES & APPLICATIONS

Published worldwide in English, Chinese, German, French, Spanish, Hungarian, Italian and other languages.

WRITTEN BY

GRANDMASTER PROF LEUNG TING

Golden Rank Founder of the International WingTsun Association,
Ph.D. in Philosophy, Guest Professor of the National Sport Academy in Bulgaria

Chief Demonstrator:
GRAND MASTER CHENG CHUEN FUN
10th Level MOC of the IWTA

ISBN: 962-7284-74-2
1st Edition: 1 Jan 2002
2nd Print: 20 Sept 2002
3rd Print: ₹1 May 2003
4th Print: 1 June 2004
5th Print: 30 Mar 2007
6th Print: 15 Nov 2010

Chief Editor
LEUNG WAI BUN
English Language Editor
JAN HUTCHINSON

www.leungting.com \ www.iwta.com

CONTENTS

About Grandmaster Professor Leung Ting

Professor **Leung Ting**, the only **Great Grandmaster** with the title of **"Golden Rank Founder"** of the **International WingTsun Association,** is also a recognized scholar with a Bachelor of Arts in Chinese and English Literature and a Doctor of Philosophy in Philosophy. In addition to these achievements, he was honored with the title "Guest Professor of Combat Arts" of the National Sport of Bulgaria in 1997.

More importantly, Prof Leung is the founder of the **Leung Ting WingTsun™ System,** a kungfu system based on traditional Chinese 詠春 *(in English "Wing Chun", "Ving Tsun" or "Wing Tsun")* but which he has adapted and improved in several ways. His system incorporates a systematic approach to teaching and a standardized grading system. It also emphasizes the application of practical fighting techniques in various situations while remaining true to the authentic concepts taught to him by the late Great Grandmaster Yip Man.

Leung Ting began studying Wing Chun at the age of 13. When he was 19 years old, he began teaching Wing Chun as a part-time "Sifu" (kungfu instructor), and at the age of 20, he became the last private student of the late Great Grandmaster Yip Man who had just "closed his door" *(retire from teaching).* From the aged Great Grandmaster, Leung learned the most advanced techniques and theories of Wing Chun.

Sifu Leung soon realized that though the techniques looked similar to what he had been taught before, the underlying concepts that he was taught by the retired grandmaster expanded and greatly changed his understanding of Wing Chun. To identify this difference in the style, Leung Ting soon registered the spelling "Wing Tsun" as the unique term for the "Wing Tsun Leung Ting Martial-Art Association Ltd." that he established in the early 70s. *(The name of this association was later changed to "International WingTsun Association" (IWTA) in the 90s and "**WingTsun™**" become the unique trademark of the Leung Ting WingTsun™ System.)*

In order to promote his new system of kungfu, Sifu Leung Ting trained hundreds of fighters to compete in various kungfu and free-fighting tournaments during

70's and early 80's. When most of his students won their matches by knocking out their opponents within one or two rounds, he was honored with the nickname **"Creator of Fighters"**. Thousands of live and televised WingTsun performances quickly made Leung Ting the "Gigantic Star of Wing Tsun" in Hong Kong and Asia. Leung Ting's name was even mentioned in the September 1972 issue of Black Belt Magazine (USA) as the "successor of Grandmaster Yip Man".

In 1976, right after his European trip, he became a technical director and planner for 24 episodes of the TV series *"Real Kungfu"* for the Rediffusion Television Station. In 1977, Mr. Chang Chieh of the Shaw Brothers Film Production Company (the topmost Kungfu movie director at that time) recruited Leung Ting to assist with his next six Kungfu movies.

After completing his contractual commitment with the Shaw Brothers, Sifu Leung Ting increased his efforts towards expanding WingTsun™ Kungfu in the Western World. He began writing books and producing documentary & instructional videotapes on kungfu for American and European martial-art enthusiasts. In the late 70's, his English edition of *Wing Tsun Kuen* was declared the "Best Chinese Kungfu Book of the decade" in the USA. In the last twenty years, this book has been translated and published in Simplified and Traditional Chinese, German, French, Spanish, Hungarian, Bulgarian, Polish, Italian, and several other languages. Today, the International WingTsun Association is the largest professional kungfu organization in the world with more than 4000 branches in over 63 countries.

Not only beginning martial-art enthusiasts are attracted to WingTsun™, thousands of experts from other martial-art styles have left their previous schools to become students in Great Grandmaster Leung Ting's schools. Some of those who have switched were high-Dan instructors while others had already earned titles in national and world championships in different martial-art tournaments worldwide.

In addition to the general WingTsun™ courses, Prof Leung designs special training programs for military and police organizations, including "Military Special Operation Personnel", "Military and Police Security Forces", and SWAT. He has trained combat-instructors for many world-wide special forces groups: such as the FBI and Marine Corps of the USA, SEK & GSG9 of Germany, NOCS of Italy,

GIP of Luxembourg, RAID of France, National Police and Anti-Terrorist Squad of India, and the Special Police units of Belgium, Austria and Spain.

Despite his remarkable achievements in bringing WingTsun™ worldwide popularity, Prof Leung is not satisfied. Currently, he is planning to re-enter the field of entertainment where he intends to further enhance the visibility of WingTsun™ with his innovative websites, **"WWW.LEUNGTING.COM"** and **"WWW.IWTA.COM"**. Because of the extensive use of video, exploring these sites will be similar to watching television shows specializing in kungfu and Chinese culture. There will be videos of great martial artists as well as interviews with famous kungfu actors and directors. There will also be shows about Feng Shui, Chi Kung, Mandarin language lessons, perhaps Chinese cooking. And for those who wish to test their own fighting abilities against those of the grandmaster, they may soon have the chance. Grandmaster Leung Ting and his business partner are designing a WingTsun™ fighting game to be included on the websites!

— *Editor*

Below: Jackie Chan was in Grandmaster Leung Ting's International Headquarters in Hong Kong when he gave an interview to an American TV crew. Could he soon be demonstrating his humorous yet challenging Kungfu techniques during an interview on *LEUNGTING.COM*?

The Background and Theory of ———

SIU-NIM-TAU

THE NAME AND ITS UNDERTONE

iu-Nim-Tau （小念頭） or literately translated as the **"Little Idea"**, is the first bare-handed kungfu set of the WingTsun system. It was formerly known to some Wing Chun people in Foshan （佛山 *or "Fat-Shan" in Cantonese*） as *"Saam-Bai-Fat"* （三拜佛） or "Praying Thrice to Buddha". It was so called because the set was previously composed of one *Tan-sau* （攤手） and two *Fook-Sau* （伏手） together with three *Wu-sau* （護手） movements which, originally known as the *"Yat-Tan, Yee-Fook, Saam-Bai-Fut"* （一攤二伏三拜佛） or literately translated as the *"Tan-sau for Once, Fook-sau for Twice and Praying to Buddha for Thrice"* sequence, in which the hand position looks as if one is praying to Buddha. However, the modern version of Siu-Nim-Tau consists of one *Tan-sau* and **three** *Fook-Sau* movements, and so would need to be called "Praying Four Times to Buddha".

Using Siu-Nim-Tau as the first kungfu set in the WingTsun discipline carries a special philosophical meaning. On a student's first day of class, the instructor will traditionally say, **"If you cannot even master a 'Little Idea' correctly, you will never do anything correctly; no matter whether you are practicing Wing Tsun or in your daily life"**. But this statement has more than just two levels of meaning.

On the simplest level, this statement refers to the fact that many of the techniques used in **Chi-Sau** （黐手） training and in real fighting are actually combinations of the basic movements from the "Little Idea" set. Therefore, if a WingTsun practitioner cannot master these basic techniques correctly, it will be difficult for him to master the correct techniques and he will not be able to fight effectively.

8

Another meaning behind "Little Idea" involves the beginner's state of mind. A new student who thinks "too much" may become distracted by too many ideas in his head and fail to understand the main point of the whole set. The name is also a caution against thinking too far ahead. A student who is preoccupied with what he will learn in the future will fail to learn what he is being taught in the present. In order to achieve larger goals, one must first fully understand each "Little Idea" that is part of the larger concept. However, This does not mean that the student is not supposed to think at all. If a student only learns the physical movements of the set and not the underlying concepts expressed within it, he has not really mastered WingTsun Kungfu. Comprehending this internal knowledge, not performing the external set is what makes a true WingTsun martial artist. This is why some people may practice for decades yet still fail to understand the essence of this martial art.

CHANGING THE TRADITIONAL CONCEPT OF MARTIAL ARTS

For a WingTsun™ practitioner, "Siu-Nim-Tau" should have yet another meaning. When first introduced, WingTsun revolutionized the concept of the traditional fighting styles of China. Traditional kungfu styles focus on using a "patterned counterattack movement" against a "patterned attack movement" under an "imaginary situation". However, in a real fighting situation, you cannot foresee what attack your opponent is going to use, and once he does attack, you do not have time to stop and think about the appropriate counterattack. Therefore, WingTsun does not emphasize "attack/counterattack" patterns, but instead focuses on being able to react and adapt to whatever attack your opponent uses. *"**Changing according to the changing of the enemy**"* is the motto of WingTsun™. Therefore, the true meaning of "Little Idea" is to advise a beginner that he must first "**totally empty his cup**" (clear his mind of preconceptions) so that he can rebuild a completely new concept starting with a "little idea".

DIFFERENT NAMES

Branches of some Wing Chun people who teach the same set call it by different names. Some call their first kungfu set **"Siu-Lin-Tau"** （小練頭） which means: *"To practice a little bit in the beginning"*. Others call it **"Siu-Lam-Tau"** （少林頭 or *"Shaolin-Tou"* in Mandarin） meaning *"Do* *not forget that Wing Chun was originated from Shaolin".* Obviously each school can express its beliefs through the name it uses; yet WingTsun™ taught in the IWTA all over the world has chosen to use the name "Siu-Nim-Tau" passed down from the late Grandmaster Yip Man as it brings out special philosophical meanings.

108 POINTS

It was said that the traditional Siu-Nim-Tau set consisted of 108 points. About such the hearsay, I could even remember during a teatime chat that Great Grandmaster Yip Man once had also mentioned about the same thing. Unfortunately, I was too reckless not to keep asking him for a detailed explanation. Years later, when I found my interest in looking for the roots of WingTsun, I began searching for the reasoning behind the 108-point-format. After extensive research, I finally discover the following explanation.

A "Single-handed movement" — any individual movement launched by one hand — is counted as "**one point**".

A "Double-handed movement" — any individual movement launched by both hands together at the same time — is counted as "**two points**".

Note: The term "individual movement" does not refer to a whole sequence of a certain movements started from the beginning to the end (e.g. withdrawal of the hand back to the flank) but to each small action within the complete technique. Say, the whole sequence from the "Double Gaun-sau" up the withdrawal of the fists would count as "eight points":

The 1st movement: the Crossed *Tan-sau* (2 points)
The 2nd movement: the Double *Gaun-sau* (2 points)
The 3rd movement: internal rotation back to the chest (2 points)
The 4th movement: Withdrawal of the hands back to the flanks (2 points)
(*Please refer to pg. 16 — 17, from Diagram #5 to #10 for details.)

THE PAST AND PRESENT

Because the present day version of Siu-Nim-Tau has been modified over the years, it no longer consists of exactly 108 points. For example, in the middle part of the old Siu-Nim-Tau set, there were two separate sequences of movements. The first sequence started from the left *Gum-sau* and ended up with Double *Lan-sau* movement right after the Double *Fat-sau* movement. The second sequence started from Double *Jum-sau* up to the Withdrawal of double-fists *(Sau-kuen)*. However, in the middle part of the current Siu-Nim-Tau, the two sections are combined together to form a non-stop succession of movements started from the Left *Gum-sau* up to the Withdrawal of double-fists. *(*See pg. 38 — 45, Diagram #81 to #105.)*

Undoubtedly, the version of Siu-Nim-Tau that was taught to the late Great Grandmaster Yip Man and the version he subsequently taught to his students are somewhat different. It is also clear that the version of Siu-Nim-Tau Great Grandmaster Yip Man taught in Foshan of Mainland China and the version that he later taught in Hong Kong are not exactly the same. However it is not clear who actually had modified the movements in the set?

WHY TRADITIONAL?

In studying kungfu or any other subject, one should try to grasp the essential concept of the material rather than dwelling too much on the origin or derivation of one or two particular points in order to show off how "genuine" or how "traditional" the material is. It is a certainly serious mistake to adhere to a stubborn and conservative attitude which leads to neglecting the distinction of "good" and "bad" as well as "right" from "wrong". It is particularly important for a WingTsun™ practitioner to iearn how to apply highly flexible and responsive techniques when fighting. When you turn out to be a loser, who cares how "traditional" you are?

STRUCTURE AND CHARACTERISTICS

One of the characteristics of the Siu-Nim-Tau set is that once after setting up the *"Yee-Gee-Kim-Yeung-Ma"* （二字拑羊馬） or "Character-Two-Adduction-Stance", the practitioner does not move his feet throughout the whole set. Maintaining this stance also strengthens legs while the student practices the hand-techniques. The simplicity of this stance has the added benefit that a WingTsun student can start learning hand-techniques the first day of class, rather than having to learn complicated stances for a certain period like the other styles before beginning to learn the hand- techniques.

11

THE IMPORTANCE OF BREATHING

When practicing Siu-Nim-Tau, it is important to breath properly, especially during the *"One Tan and Three Fook"* sequence. During this sequence, one should adopt the *"Yik-Fu-Kup"* (逆呼吸 or *"Ni-Hu-Xi"* in Mandarin) or "Reverse Breathing" method, a special way of controlling one's breathing patterns that is used in *Chi Kung* training.

During the "Reverse Breathing" one breaths in through one's nose and out through one's mouth. Also, whereas regular breathing involves only the expansion and compression of the lungs, "Reverse Breathing" involves the expansion and compression of the abdominal cavity which increases the amount of air drawn into the lungs with each breath and therefore increasing the level of oxygen absorbed by the blood.

THE ATTAINMENT OF INNER STRENGTH

If one receives quality instruction and maintains the correct stance while practicing the *"One-Tan-and-Three-Fook"* sequence, one's body will soon begin to react to this training in a specific way. One's core temperature will rise, blood vessels will expand and increase the flow of blood, and in warmer climates one will begin to sweat profusely (in cooler climates, one might begin to steam). One's breathing will also become slower and heavier. These reactions reveal that the practitioner has begun to enter into the state of "Attainment of Internal Strength" or *"Noi-Kung"* (內功) according to Chinese martial-art terminology.

Upon reaching an advanced level of "Attainment of Internal Strength", a practitioner will be able to give a "Dark-red palm" *Noi-Kung* performance by a *Tan-sau* movement. When performing the "Dark-red palm", the palm of the *Tan-sau* first turns red and then eventually purplish black and becomes much cooler than the rest of the body. When the advanced WT practitioner changes the *Tan-sau* to *Wu-sau* (Protective-arm) again, his palm will immediately return to normal skin-color and temperature. These abilities demonstrate the mystical quality of practicing Siu-Nim-Tau.

Apart from the *"One-Tan-and-Three-Fook"* sequence, all other movements in Siu-Nim-Tau should be performed at normal speed. These movements include the three palm strikes; the three elemental defending techniques (*Tan, Bong* and *Fook*); the upper, middle, and lower defending techniques, the chain-punches, and all the other movements that are included in this seemingly short, simple, and aerobic-like bare-handed kungfu set.

TO ABANDON THE FORCE, TO UNLOAD THE FORCE & TO BORROW THE FORCE

WingTsun™ emphasizes turning the opponent's own force against him. In order to successfully achieve this reversal of force, the WingTsun™ practitioner must master three essential mottoes. First he must be able to **"abandon"** his own force. Second, he must be able to **"unload"** the force of his opponent. And third, he must be able to **"borrow"** the force of his opponent in order to use it in a counterattack.

If a combatant only knows how to fight by using "power-against-power", then the stronger one will invariably win. However, once **if he regards himself "so weak" to undertake any force from his opponent, he would, instead, focus on special skills to "unload" the incoming force of his opponent. If a fighter is proficient in "unloading" an opponent's force, then no matter how strong this opponent is, he can no longer use his own power to fight against the WT practitioner, as the later actually does not even resist any incoming force.** *(The similar concept but different techniques as used by the Spanish bullfighter in fighting against a powerful charging bull.)* Finally, a masterly WingTsun™ practitioner can even "borrow" an opponent's strength to power his own counterattacks.

KEEPING THE MUSCLES RELAXED

Many people make the mistake of tensing their muscles when they launch a punch. This tension actually weakens the overall power of their punch because they are tightening both the extensor and contractor muscles. The extensor muscles are those used in launching the punch and the contractor muscles are those used in withdrawing the punch. If both sets of muscles are tense during a punch, the extensor wastes much of its power overcoming the tension of the contractor. However, if the contractor muscles are relaxed, all of the extensor muscles' power is given into the punch. This is why it is important to keep one's muscles relaxed while practicing Siu-Nim-Tau.

THE CORRECT WAY TO PRACTICE SIU-NIM-TAU

When practicing Siu-Nim-Tau, one should remain relaxed, but concentrated. The knees should be kept adducted tightly inwards, and the buttocks should be kept tucked in and tightened. The eyes should follow the movements of the hands, and one should use natural rhythmic breathing. One should also eliminate all feelings of excitement or impatience before beginning to practice.

Every movement in Siu-Nim-Tau has its unique meaning and function. It is a pity that some of the unqualified instructors may not be able to explain these things clearly to their students, and sometimes it is the student himself who is too ignorant to understand the practical applications of the movements. Therefore it is possible to spend a lifetime in practice kungfu without ever reaching the level of attainment that one strives for. As Confucius said, *"Without rational thought, one's learning will be confused"*.

In the beginning, performing Siu-Nim-Tau may feel strenuous. However, someone who receives quality instruction by a conscientious teacher, and who practices the set consistently will soon feel an increase in energy while performing Siu-Nim-Tau, and may even experience a "state of joy". These effects can be long lasting. Therefore Siu-Nim-Tau should never be considered simply an "aerobic exercise" or "only a beginner's set".

The following mottoes are helpful when practicing Siu-Nim-Tau:

Push the Head against the Sky & Stand Firmly on the Ground. (頂天立地)

Head up with Horizontal Vision. (登頭平視)

Containable Chest and Elevated Back. (涵胸拔背)

Straighten the Waist and 'Suck-in' the Abdomen. (挺腰收腹)

For all the hand movements, pay attention to:

The Sinking Elbow & Drooping Shoulder. (沈肘落膊)

When launching a hand movement:

Look where the Hand Goes. (眼隨手到)

Please also refer to the Chapters *"About the Essential Points"* and *"Mottoes in Siu-Nim-Tau"* for details.

"Little-Idea" — the First WingTsun kungfu set
SIU NIM TAU

Demonstrated by

Grandmaster Cheng Chuen Fun
(10th Level Master of Comprehension)

Setting Up the *Yee-Gee-Kim-Yeung-Ma* (1 — 4)

Relax. Stand straight, feet together, arms by your sides, hands open. Make fists and pull your arms up, tucking them close to your armpit, parallel to nipple line. Bend your knees allowing your upper body to sink vertically downward.

Using the heels as pivots, turn your feet outward as far as possible. Then using the tiptoes of your feet as pivots, turn your heels outward until both feet form an equilateral angle *(60° to each other)* on the ground. This is the **Yee-Gee-Kim-Yeung-Ma** or "Character 'Two' Adduction Stance". Make sure to keep your buttocks tucked in. (*Please refer to *"About the Essential Points"* for details)

16

Gow-cha Tan-sau — Gow-cha Gaun-sau — Kwun-sau — Sau-kuen (5 — 10) Open the hands and cross the arms, left over right, in front of your chest forming the *Gow-cha Tan-sau*. Slash both arms downwards (*Gow-cha Gaun-sau*). Then rotate the arms upwards from in-to-out (*Kwun-sau*) until they resume the Crossed *Tan-sau* again. Finally, withdraw your arms back to tucked position *(Sau-kuen).*

A: Side view of the
Gow-cha Tan-sau
(Crossed Palm-up arms)

B: Side view of the
Gow-cha Gaun-sau
(Crossed Splitting arms)

Left *Yat-gee-chung-kuen* — *Huen-sau* — *Sau-kuen* **(11 — 17)** Held the left fist vertically to resemble the Chinese character "**sun**" (日) to the center of your chest. Punch outwards, full force, along the centerline. This is the *Yat-gee-chung-kuen* (Thrusting-punch). When the arm is fully extended, open your palm upward, and circle the palm inwards (*Huen-sau*). Withdraw the fist again.

Right *Yat-gee-chung-kuen* **(or Character 'Sun' Thrusting-punch) —**
Huen-sau — Sau-kuen **(18 — 24)**
Repeat the above movement with the right hand.

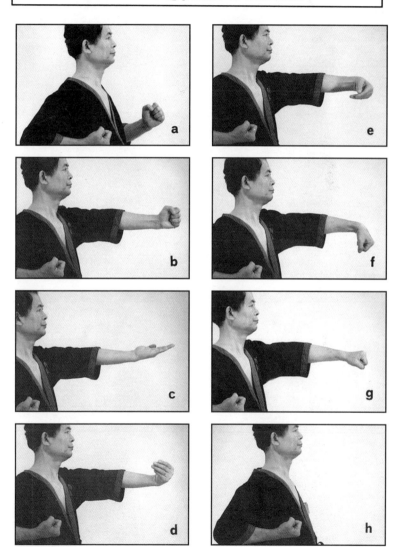

21

Tan-sau (25 — 27) Open the left palm upward and, pushing from the elbow, slowly thrust the palm forward along the Centerline until the elbow is of one fist length in front of the chest.

(*Tan-sau* 攤手 or literately translated as "Palm-up arm". Please refer to pg.74 for details)

Boon-Huen-sau — Wu-sau (28 — 31) With the **Boon-Huen-sau** or "Half Circling-hand" movement, bend the left palm inwards and circle it downwards slowly, then pull the fingers out and up until the hand is held vertically in front of the chest to form the **Wu-sau** (Protective-arm) pose. Later, withdraw the **Wu-sau** slowly until the elbow is one fist length away from the waist.

Fook-sau — Boon-Huen-sau — Wu-sau (32 — 36) Turn the palm downwards slowly to form a *Fook-sau*. Then push the arm outward along the centerline slowly until the elbow is one fist length away from the chest. Pull the fingers down, out and up (*Boon Huen-sau*) to form the *Wu-sau* again. Withdraw the hand slowly to the chest until the waist is about one-fist away from the waist.

25

2nd *Fook-sau* — *Boon-Huen-sau* — *Wu-sau* (37 — 41) Circle the hand downwards to form the *Fook-sau* again. Slowly extend the arm along the Centerline. Circle the hand to form *Wu-sau* and withdraw the hand to the chest.

3rd *Fook-sau* — *Boon-Huen-sau* — *Wu-sau* **(42 — 45)** Circle the hand downwards to form the *Fook-sau* again. Slowly extend the arm along the Centerline. Circle the hand to form *Wu-sau*, and withdraw the hand to the chest until the elbow is about one-fist distance to the waist.

Jark-cheung — Ching-cheung — Huen-sau — Sau-kuen (46 — 52) Slap the palm to the right until it reaches the width of the shoulder (*Jark-cheung*). Draw the hand back to the center of the chest and strike forward with the palm out (*Ching-cheung*). When the arm is fully extended, turn the palm upward, circle the palm inward forming a horizontal fist. Withdraw the fist.

(*About *Fook-sau* (Bridge-on Arm or Lying-on Hand), *Wu-sau* (Protective-arm) *Jark-cheung* (Sideward-palm), *Ching-cheung* (Erect-palm) and *Huen-sau* (Circling-hand), please refer to *"Application & Analysis of the Movements"* for details.)

29

Diagram a — k

Side-view illustrations of the correct posture during the sequence of *Tan-sau* (a — b), *Huen-sau* (c — e), *Wu-sau* (f — g), *Fook-sau* (h — i), *Jark-cheung* (j) and *Ching-cheung* (k). (*Note: The repetitive movements of Fook-sau and Wu-sau in these photos are omitted.*)

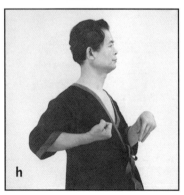

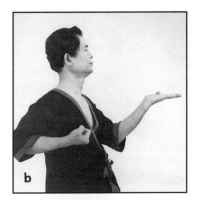

31

Tan-sau — Boon-Huen-sau — Wu-sau for the right hand (53 — 59)
Please refer to the explanation for the left hand movements.

Fook-sau — Boon-Huen-sau — Wu-sau for the right hand (60 — 64)
Please refer to the explanation for the left hand movements.

2nd *Fook-sau* — *Boon-Huen-sau* — *Wu-sau* for the right hand (65 — 68)
Please refer to the explanation for the left hand movements.

(*About *Fook-sau* (Bridge-on Arm or Lying-on Hand), *Wu-sau* (Protective-arm) *Jark-cheung* (Sideward-palm), *Ching-cheung* (Erect-palm) and *Huen-sau* (Circling-hand), please refer to *"Application & Analysis of the Movements"* for details.)

3rd *Fook-sau* — *Boon-Huen-sau* — *Wu-sau* for the right hand (69 — 72)
Please refer to the explanation for the left hand movements.

Jark-cheung (Sideward-palm) — *Ching-cheung* (Erect-palm) — *Huen-sau* (Circling-hand) — *Sau-kuen* (Withdrawal of fist) **for the right hand (73 — 80)** Please refer to the explanation for the left hand movements.

Jor Gum-sau* (81 — 82)** Slap the left palm straight down along the side of the body at full speed, until the arm is fully extended. This is the ***Jor (Left) ***Gum-sau*** (Pinning-hand) technique of WT. *(Note: When applying the Pinning-hand technique, the force should be exerted from the root of the palm.)*

Yau Gum-sau **(83 — 84)** As soon as the left arm is fully extended, slap the right palm straight down along the side of the body at full speed, until the arm is fully extended. This is the *Yau* (Right) *Gum-sau* (Pinning-hand) movement in the Siu-Nim-Tau set.

Chin Hau Gum-sau (Back and Front Pinning-hands) **(85 — 90)** Place both hands behind the back, then thrust both palms straight backwards. Bring both hands to the front of the chest, then thrust them forward and down at a slight angle.

a: Side view of the *Hau Gum-sau* (Back Pinning-hands)

b: and *Chin Gum-sau* (Front Pinning-hands)

(*Please refer to pg. 82 — 88 for details about the *Gum-sau* (Pinning-hands) movements)

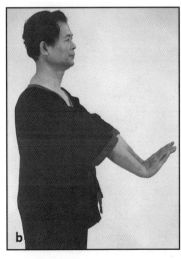

41

 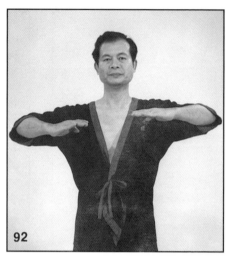

***Shang Lan-sau — Shang Fat-sau* (91 — 93)** Bend the arms and bring them to a horizontal position in front of the chest with the left arm on top of the right *(Shang Lan-sau)*. Quickly spread the arms outward to each side of the body until they are fully extended at shoulder level *(Shang Fat-sau)*.

93

Shang Lan-sau — *Shang Jum-sau* **(94 — 97)** Bring both arms into *Shang Lan-sau* (Double Bar-arms) again, with the right arm over the left. Pull the left forearm slightly inside the right, then roll both arms upward and outward until the arms are parallel to each other in from of the chest to form the *Shang Jum-sau*.

96

97

 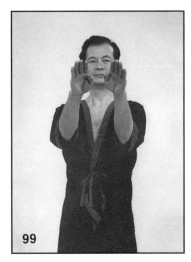

Shang Tan-Sau — Shang Jut-Sau — Shang Biu-tze-sau (98 — 101)
The elbows are slightly raised, with the both palms turned upward, forming the *Shang* (Double) *Tan-sau*. They are then turn downward, with the two arms simultaneously sinking downward quickly (**Double *Jut-sau***). On completion, thrust both arms forward with fingers straighten with **Double *Biu-tze-sau***.

Cheong-Kiu Gum-sau — Shang Tai-sau — Sau-kuen (102 — 105)

Changed to *Cheong-kiu Gum-sau* (Long-Bridge Pinning-hands) by exerting the force from the shoulders to press both palms downward. Then raise the fully-extended-arms vertically by the force of the shoulders. Withdraw the arms.

Diagram a — k:

Side views of *Shang Lan-sau* through Withdrawal of fists. Please note that in all of the "Short Bridge-arm" movements, the force is exerted from the elbows, whereas during the "Long Bridge-arm" movements *Cheong-kiu Gum-sau* (Long-bridge Pinning-hands) and *Shang Tai-sau* (Double Lifting-arms), in which the arms are straight and the joints are locked, the force is exerted from the shoulders. *(Please refer to pg.92 — 100)*

46

47

Jark-cheung — Wang-cheung **(106 — 109)** Slap the left palm to the right until it reaches the sideline of shoulder. Withdraw the palm to the center of the chest. Turn the palm down to form the *Wang-cheung* (Lying-palm) pose and thrust it forward until the arm is fully extended.

Huen-sau — Sau-kuen (110 — 113)

Turn the palm up, curl it upwards and circle it inwards into a fist. Withdraw the hand to the side of the chest.

Right *Jark-cheung* (Sideward-palm) — ***Wang-cheung*** (Lying-palm) — ***Huen-sau*** (Circling-hand) — ***Sau-kuen*** (Withdrawal of Fist) **(114 — 121)** Repeat the previous sequence with the right hand.

Tan-sau — ***Jum-sau*** — ***Gwat-sau*** **(122 — 125)** Push the left arm out quickly along the Centerline and make a ***Tan-sau*** pose. Change to ***Jum-sau*** by lowering the elbow and sinking the palm a few inches downward. Then change to ***Gwat-sau*** by swiping the arm downward in a clockwise curve till the hand is in front of the outside edge of the left thigh.

Lau-sau — *Ko Tan-sau* — *Dai-cheung* (126 — 131) Turn the left palm up and lift the forearm upward *(Lau-sau)* until the palm is at ear level (*Ko Tan-sau*). Circle the hand clockwise until it is horizontally palm out and immediately lower it until the hand reaches waist level (*Dai-cheung*).

130

131

Huen-sau — Sau-kuen **(132 — 136)** Turn the left hand palm-up while keeping it at the lower abdominal position. Then circle the hand clockwise into a fist. Finally withdraw the fist to the armpit.

134

135

(*About *Gwat-sau* (Wiping-arm), *Lau-sau* (Scooping-arm), *Ko Tan-sau* (High Palm-up arm) and *Dai-cheung* (Lower Lying-palm), please refer to pg. 101 — 106 for details)

Right *Tan-sau* (Palm-up arm) — *Gwat-sau* (Wiping-arm) — *Lau-sau* (Scooping-arm) — *Dai-cheung* (Lower Lying-palm) and *Sau-kuen* (Withdrawal of the fist) **(137 — 149)** Using the right hand to repeat the sequence described previously.

140

141

144

145

57

146

147

148

149

Diagram a — h:
Side views of the sequence *Tan-sau* (Palm-up arm), *Jum-sau* (Sinking-arm), *Gwat-sau* (Wiping-arm), *Lau-sau* (Scooping-arm), *Ko Tan-sau* (High Palm-up arm), *Dai-cheung* (Lower Lying-palm), *Huen-sau* (Circling-hand) and *Sau-kuen* (Withdrawal of the fist).

f

150

g

h

153

Bong-sau — Tan-sau — Ong-cheung **(150 — 154)** Turn the elbow of the left arm up and open the left hand palm-down. Swing the elbow to the Centerline to make a *Bong-sau* posture. Lower the elbow to the chest and flip the hand palm up forming *Tan-sau*. Extend the fingers downward and thrust outward along the Centerline, until the arm is fully extended (*Ong-cheung*).

Tan-sau — Huen-sau — Sau-kuen **(155 — 158)** Lift the left hand into *Tan-sau*. Circle the hand and withdraw the fist.

Right *Bong-sau* (Wing-arm) **—** *Tan-sau* (Palm-up arm) **—** *Ong-cheung* (Reverse-palm) **(159 — 164)** Perform the sequence with the right arm as previously described.

Right *Tan-sau* (Palm-up arm) — *Huen-sau* (Circling-hand) — *Sau-kuen* (Withdrawal the fist) **(165 — 169)** Using the right hand, repeat the sequence previously described.

166

Diagram a — f: Side views ⟹
of the sequence from *Bong-sau* to
Ong-cheung. Note that *Bong-sau*
should be performed by first lifting up
the elbow before swinging it forwards.

169

a

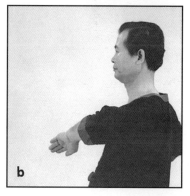

b

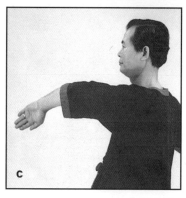

c

d

e

f

170

Note: The force of palm-strikes is exerted from the elbow and is finally focused through the root of the palm.

173

***Tut-sau* (170 — 172)** Extend the left arm diagonally in front of the abdomen with palm facing inward. Place the right hand palm-up against the elbow joint of the left arm. Slide the right palm downward along the left arm while drawing the left arm up until the left hand rests palm-up against the right elbow.

176 177

Tut-sau (continued) **(173 — 174)** With the right arm extended diagonally in front of the abdomen, slide the left palm downward along the right arm while drawing the right arm up until the right hand rests palm-up against the left elbow. Slide the right palm downward along the left arm while drawing the left arm up until the left hand forms a fist in front of the chest.

180 181

Lin-Wan Chung-kuen — Sau-sik **(176 — 178)** Launch a left punch along the Centerline. When the arm is fully extended, immediately punch the right fist outward along the Centerline while drawing back the left fist under the right arm until it is close to the chest. Do this for several times at high speed (*Lin-Wan Chung-kuen*). Finally do *Huen-sau* as a *Sau-sik* (Ending) movement.

Diagram a — h: Side views of the sequence from *Tut-sau* (Freeing Hands) to *Lin-wan Chung-kuen* (Chain-punches). Please note the distance between the arms and the body.

APPLICATION & ANALYSIS OF THE MOVEMENTS
GOW-CHA GAUN-SAU (交叉揆手 or Crossed Splitting-block)

The Crossed *Gaun-sau* is a "double-movement" in the set, it is actually two lower Gaun-sau performed at the same time. In practical application it should be used separately and combined with other appropriate techniques.

The Lower *Gaun-sau* is normally used in combination with the "Character 'SUN' Thrusting-punch" *(or "Thrusting-punch" in short)* ∗ in order to deflect a mid-or-lower level attack and simultaneously counterattack. In addition, the Lower *Gaun-sau* is generally used with the body turning slightly sideway so as to maximize its effectiveness. For instance, when the left *Gaun-sau* is used, the body should be turned slightly to the left, so that an attack by the opponent can be evaded. This sideways evasion is particularly important when deflecting a kick.

Demonstrators: **Sifu Lau Ka Sun** (Left)
Sifu Yen Yiu Wing (Right)

⇧

COMMON MISTAKE:

The demonstrator had both arms bent, thus failing to protect the groin. Also his arms and hands are placed too close to his body. From this position he could not react quickly enough to block a punch or kick from his opponent.

72

Example a — c

A (left) and B (right) facing each other. When B initiates a right punch at A's mid-lower level, A immediately executes a right diagonally downward smash from above B's right punch. At the same time A dissolves B's punch, A's left "Character 'SUN' Thrusting-punch" has already landed on B's face.

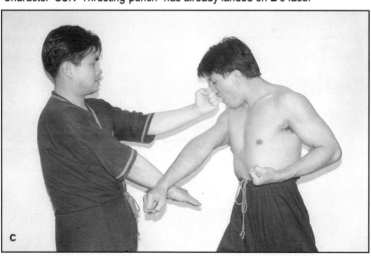

TAN-SAU (攤手 or **Palm-up Arm**)

The *Bong-sau, Tan-sau* and *Fook-sau*, commonly called *"Bong, Tan* and *Fook"* in short, are collectively known as the three fundamental moves in WingTsun.

In the first section of Siu-Nim-Tau, when practicing the *"One Tan and Three Fook"* sequence, the practitioner is required to execute the movements slowly. The sequence should also be performed with the deep, slow and rhythmic breathing. That is the essence of *Chi Kung* (Breath Training).

Tan-sau can be further classified into "Crossed *Tan-sau*", "Mid *Tan-sau*" and "High *Tan-sau*". The Crossed *Tan-sau* is commonly used as a transitional move, such as when it is performed at the beginning of Siu-Nim-Tau, before the execution of Crossed *Gaun-sau*. The Mid *Tan-sau* is the most commonly used technique. Thus when the term *"Tan-sau"* is used without a modifier, it usually means Mid *Tan-sau*. In combat situations *Tan-sau* can be applied in a vast variety of ways. The High *Tan-sau* is mostly used as a counterattack to the roundhouse punch or high roundhouse kick.

EXAMPLES OF *TAN-SAU* COMBINED WITH OTHER TECHNIQUES:
1. *Tan-sau and a counterpunch from the outside ("Outdoor Area") (Diagram a — c)*
2. *Tan-sau and a counterpunch from the inside. (Pg. 76 Upper Diagram)*
3. *Tan-sau from the inside with an "Arm-pressing Punch" from the outside. (Pg. 76 Lower Diagram)*

Tan-sau can be combined with various movements such as palm-strikes, Low *Bong-sau*, and other punches and kicks, in both Chi-Sau drills and real fighting situations.

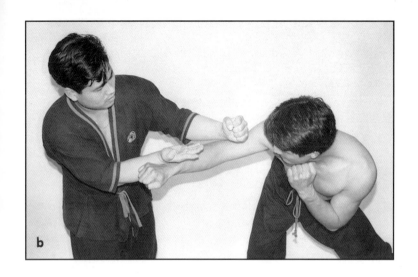

Diagram a — c

When **B** (right) launches a jab to attack **A** (left), **A** immediately applies a right *Tan-sau* and turns his body to the right to nullify **B**'s powerful punch. At the same time, **A** launches a left Thrusting-punch to attack **B**'s head.

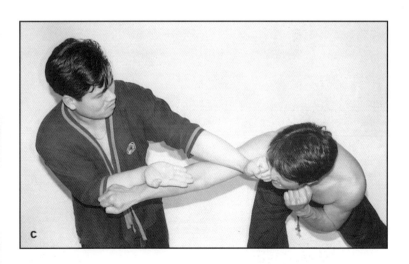

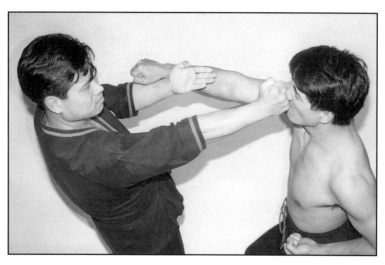

Above:
Both *Tan-sau* and "Character 'Sun' Thrusting-punch" from inside

Below:
A *Tan-sau* from inside with an "Arm-pressing Punch" from outside

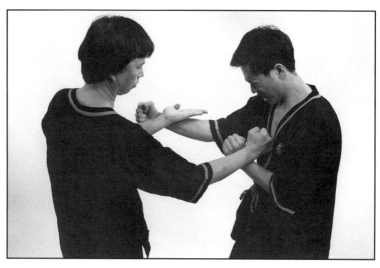

YAT-GEE-CHUNG-KUEN (日字衝拳 or Character 'SUN' Thrusting Punch), UN-WAN-KUEN (連環拳 or Chain-punches) & BIK-BO-TIP-DA (迫步貼打 or "Close-Range Pursuing–Attack" Tactic)

The "Character 'SUN' Thrusting-punch", also called the "Straight-line Thrusting-punch" or just "Thrusting-punch" in short, is the most important punching technique of the WingTsun system. In accordance with the principle *"a straight line is the shortest distance between two points"*, the "Thrusting Punch" not only follows a straight line but also follows the ***"Shortest Straight Line"*** (the Center line) between the two opposing fighters. *(Please refer to Pg. 129)*

Almost all other martial art styles teach people to pause between punches, so that, if the opponent evades the first punch, the attacker has to first draw back his punch before making a second punch. This style of fighting is similar to firing a single shot pistol *(i.e. After each shot, the pistol must be re-cocked before it will fire again allowing the enemy a chance to run away)*.

WingTsun emphasizes the use of "Chain Punches", a rapid-fire technique where one continuously punches and advances towards the enemy making it impossible for him to back out of range of the attack. This tactic is called "**Close Range Pursuing Attack**". Thus the WingTsun style of fighting is similar to chasing after the enemy with a machine gun.

Other WingTsun techniques combine the "Thrusting Punch" with different hand-techniques such as *Gaun-sau, Tan-sau, Fook-sau, Gwat-sau* and others in order to dissolve an opponent's attack and counterattack simultaneously.

Right Diagram:
Prof Leung Ting demonstrating the "**Close Range Pursuing Attack**" which continuously presses the opponent making it nearly impossible to defend himself.

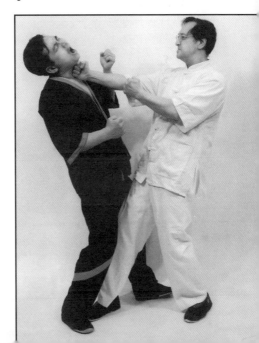

FOOK-SAU (伏手 or **Bridge-on Arm** or **Lying-on Hand**)

Fook-sau, which literately means "one's hand is lying on the wrist of one's opponent", is one the three fundamental hand-techniques in the WingTsun system. The relationship between *Fook-sau* and *Tan-sau* is that *Fook-sau* lies on top of *Tan-sau* during *Poon-Sau* (盤手 or "Rolling Arms") training in Double-armed Chi-Sau drill. Thus the relationship between *Fook-sau* and *Tan-sau* is quite delicate since these two hand-techniques control each other yet deviate from each other under certain conditions.

When doing *Fook-sau* during the *Siu-Nim-Tau* set, the practitioner should feel tension in the forearm. This exercise helps strengthen the muscles of the forearm, so that they will be able to provide the bursting strength known as "Long-Bridge-Force" or "Explosive Power" *(some other martial artists call it the "Inch-power").* This is the power that enables a WingTsun expert to produce a powerful punch while moving the arm only an extremely short distance.

In Chi-Sau drills or in real fighting, *Fook-sau* does not take the shape of a hook as performed in Siu-Nim-Tau. It is done with the palm of one's hand sticking lightly to the wrist of the opponent. From this position, the WingTsun practitioner can change the *Fook-sau* into a *Gum-sau* (Pinning-hand) movement by pressing down on his opponent's wrist, or a *Jut-sau* (Jerking-hand) movement by jerking his opponent's wrist to pull his opponent off balance.

Fook-sau can also be transformed into other techniques in order to respond appropriately to the actions of the opponent. Say, it can be changed into a *Biu-tze-sau* by thrusting out the arm swiftly to attack the opponent on the eye; or transforming to the "Grappling-hand" so as to control and attack the opponent simultaneously. By turning the palm vertically, it becomes a *Jum-sau;* or by turning the palm up to become a *Tan-sau* and so forth.

**Diagram
a — c**

When **B** (left) launches a left Thrusting-punch towards **A**'s (right) mid-level, **A** immediately counters with a left *Fook-sau* on the opponent's left wrist. **A** then changes his *Fook-sau* to a *Jut-sau* movement by suddenly pressing down **B**'s left wrist. At the same time, **A** punches **B**'s chest with a right Thrusting-punch.

Demonstrators:
  Sifu Yang Kai Kwong (Right)   **Lee Wing Ho** (Left)

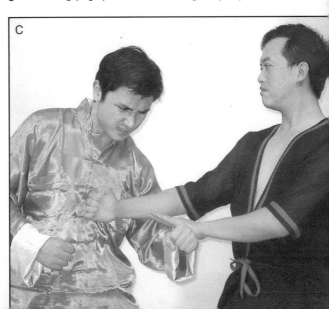

JARK-CHEUNG (側拿 or **Sideward palm**)

The "Sideward-palm" or "Sideward Slapping-hand" is a movement converted from a *Wu-sau* posture. The Sideward-palm serves the same function as the Slapping-hand in the Chum-Kiu set but to a different direction. In a combat situation, the Sideward-palm is mostly used as a second line of defense.

WingTsun Kungfu normally does **NOT** endorse the *"Block First and then Attack"* fighting method. When a fighter allows his opponent to attack first, he is allowing his opponent to gain the initiative in the fight. In such a situation, even if the fighter is able to neutralize the first attack, he is still only reacting to his opponent's attack and not controlling the fight. Meanwhile, his enemy has probably launched the second attack.

Since it is unlikely that his opponent will stop attacking once he has the initiative, the fighter will be forced to continually defend himself and will not be able to launch his own attacks. *(In a real fight, nobody can withstand a series of attacks without getting hit by at least one of them. Unless, of course, he is in the movies, or his opponent suffers from severe vision problems!)*

This is the reason WingTsun focuses on techniques where one can **"Defend and Attack Simultaneously"**. Using these techniques, one can achieve the "dreaming effect" described by Chinese martial artists with the following saying: ***"Start later, yet reach the target earlier"***.

The following photographs depict a simultaneous defense and counterattack using a Sideward-palm with a Thrusting-punch.

a

Demonstrators:

Sifu Yeung Kai Kwong
(Right)
Assistant Instructor
Wolfgang Bremer
(Left)

Diagram a — c

B initiates a jab attack towards **A**'s head. When the punch reaches the range of **A**'s extended right arm, instead of stepping back, **A** advances a step towards his opponent, applying a left Sideward-palm to block **B**'s oncoming punch, while counterattacking with a right Thrusting-punch to **B**'s face.

JOR YAU GUM-SAU
(左右撳手 or Left & Right Pinning-hand)

Practicing these movements in Siu-Nim-Tau not only to improve the striking power of Stamping-palms, it also has a practical combat application. WT incorporates a rare counter-fighting technique called "*Bok-Da*" (膊打 or "**Shoulder-strike**"). It involves ramming one's shoulder into the opponent's chest. However, the source of the striking-power in the shoulder-strike does not essentially come from the shoulder but rather from the Side-step crashing into the legs of the opponent though the movement comes from the side Pinning-hand movements.

Diagram a — d
B twists **A**'s arm. **A** suddenly extends his arm downward with a Side-step, which nullifies the arm-lock and simultaneously strikes **B** in the chest with the shoulder. **A** continues to attack **B** with a left Thrusting-punch.

COMMON MISTAKE:
The arms too far from the body, thus losing the meaning of the proper method in Shoulder-strike.

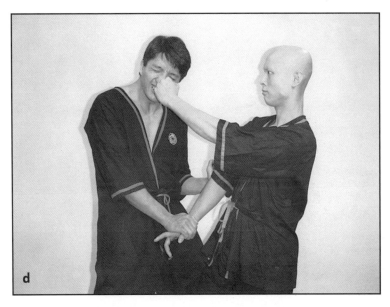

83

HAU GUM-SAU (後撤手 or **Backward Pinning hand**)

It is the only rearward attack in the WingTsun system and is regarded as a "tricky movement" or a "surprise attack" against one's opponent.

Normally WingTsun emphasizes the **"Face to Face Pursuing Attack"** tactic; therefore most techniques are formulated for frontal attack and defense. *"Exposing the back"* to the opponent is generally considered unwise according to WingTsun principles, since exposing one's back allows the opponent an ideal opportunity to attack. However under certain circumstance, when a WingTsun practitioner must expose his back to his opponent, this movement will be extremely effective.

When one's arm is being twisted backward, the *Hau Gum-sau* can be very useful. In this situation, one suddenly turns in the direction of the twisted arm until one's back is towards the opponent, then one uses the *Hau Gum-sau* to strike the opponent's floating ribs. This attack will hurt the opponent seriously and force him to let go. After using the *Hau Gum-sau,* one should turn quickly to face the opponent and continue the attack.

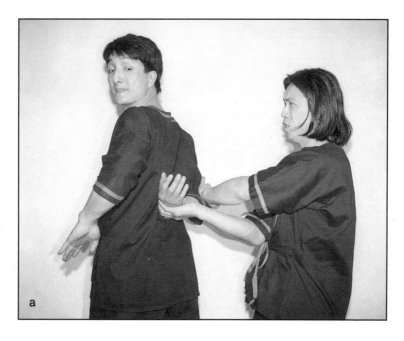

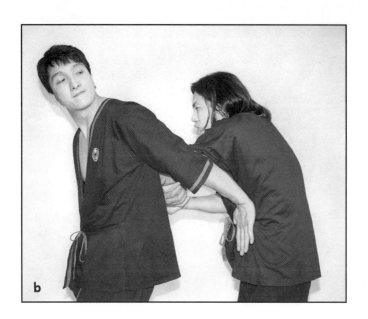

Diagram a – e

B (right) twists A's right arm backwards with an arm-lock. A suddenly turns his back clockwise so he can apply a left *Gum-sau* striking towards B's lowest rib. In great pain, B is forced to let go of A. At this moment A immediately turns back to the "face to face" position, thrusting his left leg into B's stance and launching a Thrusting-punch in B's face.

Demonstrators:

Sifu Ngan Tak Yee
Sifu Yan Yiu Wing

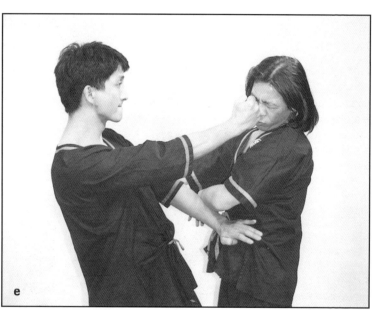

CHIN GUM-SAU (前撳手 or **Front Pinning-hand**)

Since the types of *Gum-sau* that are performed in the middle of the *Siu-Nim-Tau* set are not frequently seen in combat situations, many Wing Chun people ignore them. Some people even think that these movements are only included in order to develop the strength of palm-strikes, or increase the flexibility in the shoulders and arms. This, of course, is a misconception. For example, the front *Gum-sau* can be used as a type of palm-strike attack generally using both hands in order to increase its destructive power.

Above: Professor Leung Ting demonstrates the different positions of the two movements

(Top left) The **Front Gum-sau** is a "double-palm strike" towards the abdominal area of the opponent. Therefore the palms should be held vertically.

(Top right) The **Long-bridge Gum-sau** is a defending technique. When the movement is completed the palms should lie horizontally in front of the abdomen.

Demonstrators:
Sifu Fong Bing Yiu (Left)   Assistant Instructor **Bjoern Fandelin** (Right)

Diagram 1 — 3

B (left) attacks **A** with a double-punch. **A** blocks his attack with a Double *Jut-sau*, which causes **B** to lose his balance and fall forward. **A** immediately

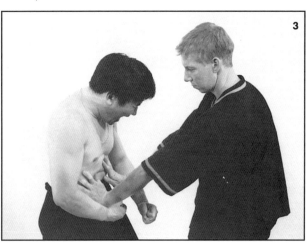

attacks **B** in the abdomen with a Double Front *Gum-sau* strike.

LAN-SAU (攔手 or **Bar-arm**) & FAT-SAU (拂手 or **Whisking-arm**)

The strength generated during the transformation from *Lan-sau* to *Fat-sau* is subtle, swift, and extremely powerful. It is as if your arms were two rattan canes being bent towards each other. When the tension is suddenly released, the rattan canes spring apart with an extremely fast motion because of their resilience.

When one is using *Fat-sau*, one is not restricted to striking only with the edge of the hands. With the correct exertion of power, the upper arms, elbows, forearms, wrists, and even fingers can be used to attack opponents. In practical usage, it can be performed with one arm or both arms to attack opponents on one or both sides.

Left:
If the arms of the *Fat-sau* are too high, too low or uneven, the exertion of strength will be uneven, and they will miss the correct attacking position towards the neck of the opponent.

Above and Below: Two common mistakes of *Fat-sau* movement

Right:
Some people withdraw the *Fat-sau* too quickly, before the arms are fully extended. This is like braking a car before it reaches the desired speed.

Below: A Single *Fat-sau* demonstrated by Grandmaster Leung Ting in application

Diagram a — c

A is aware that he is positioned in the middle of two opponents, and that if both of them attack him at the same time, he will have no room to withdraw. Under these circumstances, A immediately uses a Double *Fat-sau* to attack both of them before they can attack him. Since *Fat-sau* operates with bursting speed and power, and the throat is one of the weakest points on the human body, once the opponents get hit, they lose their ability to attack and are defeated in one move. "***Attack is the Best Defense***" is one of the concepts of WingTsun fighting tactic.

Demonstrators: **Sifu Chung Sai Wing** (Middle)
Sifu Chan Yuen Wai (Left)
Sifu Yan Yiu Wing (Right)

LAN (攔 or **Bar-arm**) — **JUM** (扰 or **Sinking-block**) — **TAN** (攤 or **Palm-up Arm**) — **JUT** (窒 or **Jerking-hand**) & **BIU-TZE-SAU** (標指手 or **Thrusting-fingers**)

The techniques, Double *Lan-sau* – Double *Jum-sau* – Double High *Tan-sau* – Double *Jut-sau* and Double *Biu-tze-sau,* which are performed in sequence during Siu-Nim-Tau, are all regarded as "Double-handed movements".

In a fight, the complete sequence can be used as a combination attack, or each individual technique can be used on its own. The double *Jut-sau* is commonly used in Chi-Sau drills. When both of one's arms are pinned on the "Outdoor Area" *(Note)* of the opponent's wrists, one can use *Jut-sau* to suddenly press down both forearms of the opponent, causing the opponent to lose balance and fall forward. This presents a good opportunity to attack the opponent's eyes with *Biu-tze-sau. (Note: Please refer to pg.129)*

Diagrams **A** to **F** as in *pg. 93* and *pg. 94* is the application of the "one-handed movement" of the **Jum-sau**, **Jut-sau** and **Biu-tze-sau** sequence combined with the **Boon-Huen-sau** (Half Circling-hand) and **Ching-cheung** (Erect-palm strike) demonstrated by Grandmaster Leung Ting and Sifu Lau Ga Sun.

Below Left: Double *Tan-sau* demonstrated by the late Grand Master Yip Man
Below Right: Double *Jut-sau* demonstrated by the late Grand Master Yip Man

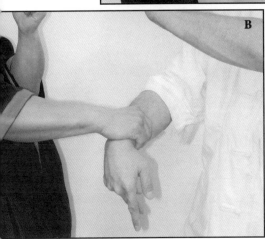

Diagrams A — C:
Application of the middle section combined with *Boon Huen-sau* & Erect-palm strike:
B grabs **A**'s right wrist with his right hand. **A** applies the *Huen-sau* movement to circle his hand and rotates his forearm clockwise until it presses down on **B**'s wrist.

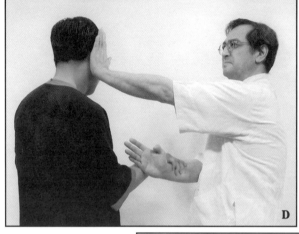

Diagrams D — F:
Simultaneously **A** launches an Erect-palm to hit **B** on the ear. As **B**'s wrist is twisted and his ear gets hurt, he is forced to let go.

A then uses his left hand to press **B**'s wrist downward with a *Jut-sau* movement and attacks **B**'s eye with his right thumb by a *Biu-tze-sau* strike. Meanwhile **A** continues to control **B**'s right arm to keep **B** from escaping.

KO *TAN-SAU* (高攤手 or **High Palm-up arms**) —
　SHANG JUT-SAU (雙窒手 or **Double Jerking Hand**) —
　　BIU-TZE-SAU (標指手 or **Thrusting-fingers**) —
　　　CHEONG-KIU GUM-SAU (長橋撳手 or **Long-bridge Pinning-hand**) —
　　　　SHANG TAI-SAU (雙提手 or **Double Lifting-arm**)

The movements in the above sequence are all 'Double-handed movements''. However, in a combat situation, this sequence can be applied using only one hand. Furthermore, each technique can be used individually or left out of the sequence depending on the situation. This conforms to the WingTsun mottoes, **"No fixed movement"** and **"Changing According to the Changing of the Opponent"**. The following sequence serves as an example.

Diagram a — f
B (left) grabs **A**'s wrists with both hands. **A** quickly rotates his forearms into High *Tan-sau position*, which twists **B**'s wrists causing him to let go. **A** then uses the Double *Jut-sau* to press down **B**'s arms, causing **B** to lose his balance and fall forward, **A** takes advantage of the fall to hit **B** in the chin with the "Double Lifting-arm" movement. Since the chin is a weak point on the human body, **B** could be knocked out instantly.

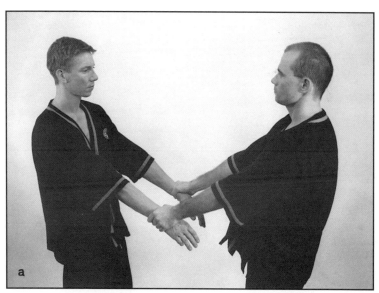

96

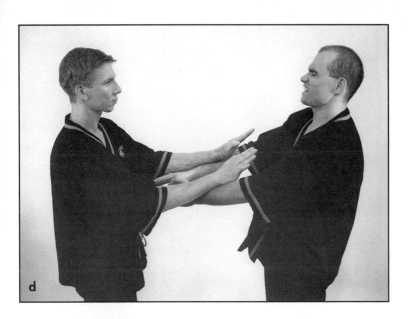

97

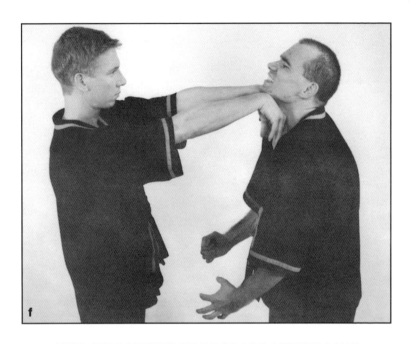

f

LONG-BRIDGE PINNING-HANDS & DOUBLE LIFTING-ARMS

In "short-bridge-arm" movements *(movements where the arm is bent and close to the practitioner's body)* the force is normally exerted from the elbows, as in *Jut-sau, Gum-sau, and Jum-sau.* WingTsun practitioners call this *"Jarn-Dai-Lak"* (睜底力) or "*power from the bottom of the elbow*" which actually means, "the force exerted from the triceps" (extensor).

However, if a WT practitioner's elbows are being lifted up while his arms are totally extended, he cannot exert his power from the elbows. Under these conditions, all he can use is the "Long-bridge Pinning-hands" technique. This technique uses the weight of the whole upper body focused through the shoulders and into the hands to generate a sudden extremely strong downward pressure. This sudden downward pressure causes the opponent to lose his balance and fall forward. Not only does this alleviate the danger of having one's elbows lifted, it can turn a losing situation into a winning one.

Diagram 1 — 4: Turning a Losing situation into a Winning one by a Recovery Movement

A (right) attacks **B** with a Double Thrusting-punch to the face, but are nullified by **B** using Double Lifting-hands at the elbows. With both arms fully extended, **A** is in an extremely disadvantageous position. **A** immediately applies the Long-bridge Pinning-hands as a recovery technique, causing **B** to lose balance and fall forward. **A** lifts both arms in a violent motion, hitting **B** in the chin with his wrists.

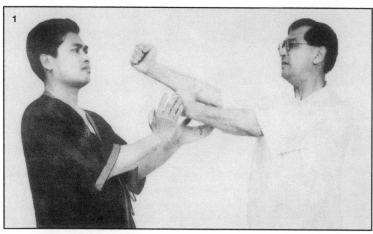

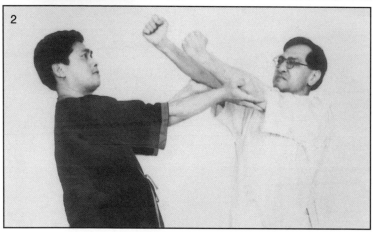

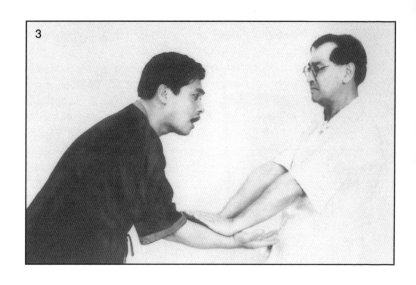

Demonstrators:
Grandmaster Leung Ting (Right)
Sifu Lau Ka Sun (Left)

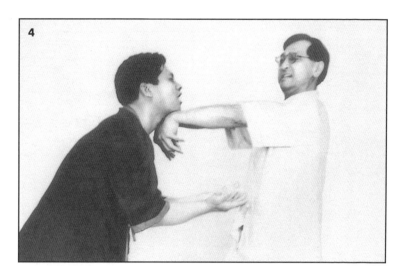

JUM-SAU (扰手 or **Sinking-block**) — GWAT-SAU (刮手 or **Wiping-arm**) — LAU-SAU (捞手 or **Scooping-arm**) — KO TAN-SAU (高攤手 or **High Tan-sau**)

The above movements can be used in combat either as a combined sequence or as individual techniques. ***Tan-sau*** and ***Jum-sau*** are both techniques for dissolving attacks to the mid-level. However, *Tan-sau* is used to dissolve an attack coming over one's arm. Whereas, *Jum-sau* is used to dissolve an attack coming under one's arm.

Both ***Gwat-sau*** and ***Gaun-sau*** are techniques for dissolving attacks to the mid-lower level of the body. They look very similar yet differ in position and function. *Gwat-sau* is performed by swinging the arm down and out in a circular movement until the arm stops in front of the outer edge of the thigh. It is mainly used to counter the roundhouse kick, and is always combined with the following "*Lau-sau*" movement so as to hold the opponent's leg with the arm joint. *Gaun-sau* is performed by moving the arm down and out in a straight diagonal line.

Strictly speaking, *Gaun-sau* is a "striking-back" movement rather than a "dissolving" movement. When correctly performed, *Gaun-sau* has the lashing power of a thick rattan cane and will cause the opponent a great deal of pain, destroying his will to fight.

The late Great Grandmaster Yip Man Demonstrating Gaun-sau (left) and Gwat-sau (right)

101

Application of *Gwat-sau* and *Lau-sau*

Diagram a — b

A (Left) stands in the WT pre-fighting posture facing **B**. **B** suddenly rushes towards **A** and attacks him with a roundhouse-kick. Instead of stepping backwards, **A** darts into **B**'s stance. This is a unique fighting strategy in WingTsun that makes the attacker misjudge the distance between himself and his target. *(See Note below.)*

Note:

When sparring with an opponent who is noted for his kicking skill, the average fighter subconsciously tends to keep a certain distance from his opponent.

This is in fact the opposite of what one should do. Since legs are longer than arms, keeping one's distance actually gives a good kicker the most advantageous range for attacking.

It should be noted that: "the closer one can get to his opponent; the harder it is for his opponent to apply kicking attacks". At close range, the hands are always the most effective weapons, since the fist, palms, fingers, shoulders and elbows can all be used at will.

Diagram c — e
(Continue)

At the same time **A** darts into **B**'s stance, he turns slightly and applies a *Gwat-Sau* by winging his right arm downward to deflect **B**'s kick. **A** immediately changes his *Gwat-Sau* to a *Lau-sau* and "scoops" **B**'s leg onto his arm, lifting it up. At the same time, **A** counterattacks using a Throat-cutting Hand.

Demonstrators:
    Sifu Lau Ka Sun (Right)
    Sifu Ngan Tak Yee (Left)

Diagram f — g:
(Continue)
A continues to step in with both arms extended throwing the injured **B** to the ground.

KO TAN-SAU (高攤手 or **High Palm-up arm**)

In addition to the Crossed *Tan-sau* discussed earlier, there are several other variations of *Tan-sau* including the Mid *Tan-sau* and the High *Tan-sau* (Please also refer to the sections on *"Bong-sau and Reverse-Palm"* and *"Tan-sau"*). These two variations are entirely different in both positioning and utility.

The High *Tan-sau* is commonly used to block attacks such as the hook-punch, roundhouse punch, whipping back-fist, or even high roundhouse kick and so forth.

The High *Tan-sau* is most effective when combined with an advancing diagonal step towards the opponent with a sideways posture. Once a WingTsun practitioner has mastered this technique, he can greatly diminish the impact of his opponent's punches, because at such close range, his opponent's punches will not have much power. *(No one can hit his own face with a roundhouse punch).*

Diagram 1 — 3: High Tan-sau used to counter a roundhouse punch

B (left) launches a right roundhouse punch at **A**'s temple. **A** steps in, turns to face B, and uses a High *Tan-sau* to dissolve B's punch while attacking B's face with a Thrusting-punch.

105

BONG-SAU (膀手 or **Wing-arm**) & ONG-CHEUNG (昂拿 or **Reverse -palm**)

Bong-sau is the first among the "Three Elemental Techniques" of WingTsun. However, since WingTsun adheres to the motto of "attack and defend at the same time" and *Bong-sau* is a nullifying technique, it is rarely applied except in specific circumstances. *(Please refer to Pg. 108)*

However, if an opponent attacks a WingTsun practitioner by pressing his arm downward, he should automatically rotate his elbow upward to form the *Bong-sau*. This conforms to one of the mottoes about the formation of *Bong-sau*: "When the head is pressed down, the tail raises up".

Bong-sau should be as flexible and resilient as rattan. It should bend to the pressure of an oncoming attack, but still keep a certain distance between the attacking fist and the practitioner's body. Therefore, no matter how powerful the attacker is, his power will be mostly "absorbed" by the elastic force of the *Bong-sau*. Once the *Bong-sau* is bent downward steeply enough, the forearm acts like a slide, and the downward pressure is totally "unloaded". *(Diagram A and B)*

In the *Siu-Nim-Tau* taught by Great Grandmaster Yip Man in Hong Kong, the "Reverse Stamping-palm" (or just "Reverse-palm") is performed towards the upper mid-level position of the opponent. He believed that this was the more difficult angle to strike with force, and felt that it was important for his students to learn this more difficult attack. In real fighting, "Reverse-palm" glides over the arm of the opponent to strike his mid-lower position.

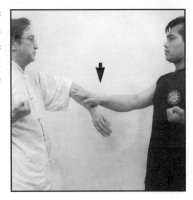

BONG-SAU IS NOT AN ALL-PURPOSE DEFENDING TECHNIQUE!

In spite of the importance of *Bong-sau*, it should be noted that in most fights, it is often "not necessary" or even "not suitable" to apply *Bong-sau*. In the following examples, a WingTsun fighter can defeat his opponent by fighting according to the tactics: **"Defend and Attack Simultaneously"** *(Diagram A)* or **"to counter an attack by an attack"** *(Diagram B)*. If *Bong-sau* were consistently used, it would have

a totally negative effect, and one would undoubtedly get hit by the opponent.

Diagram A:
Defend a mid-level straight punch and attack with a *Tan-sau* and a Thrusting-punch simultaneously.

Diagram B:
If an opponent launches a jab at a WT fighter's face, he only needs to counterattack using a Thrusting-punch to the face of the opponent and a Sideward-palm for protection at the same time.

Diagram
a — f:

When **B** (right) launches a left Thrusting-punch at **A**, **A** immediately extends his left arm to receive the punch. **B**'s punch is so powerful that makes **A** bend his left arm into *Bong-sau*. **A** redirects the force using the turning stance. **A** turns back his body towards **B**'s left flank immediately and immobilizes **B**'s arm with a Pinning-hand. Simultaneously **A** lands a Reverse-palm at the waist of his opponent.

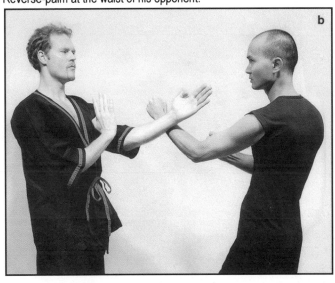

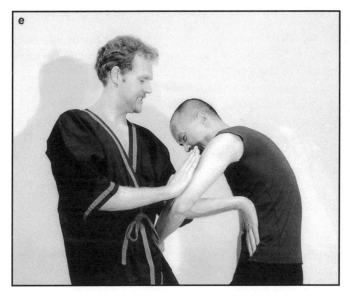

Demonstrators: **Sifu Chung Sai Wing** (left)
                Sifu Brandon Rhea (right)

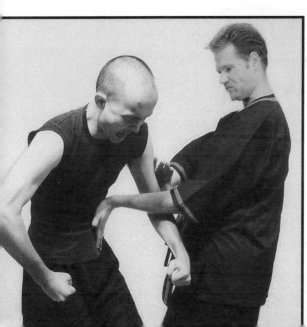

**Opposite-side
View**

TUT-SAU (脱手 or **Arm-freeing**) & CHUNG-KUEN (衝拳 or **Thrusting-punch**)

Tut-sau and Thrusting-punch are two different movements in Siu-Nim-Tau. However, they can be combined to form a technique used to neutralize a grab and launch an attack at the same time.

In general, *Tut-sau* is not considered a very clever technique, since it is unlikely that an opponent would be able to grapple a WingTsun practitioner's hand. However, it is a traditional movement, and I do not see any benefit in abandoning it. Even though to escape a grappling attack against one hand, all you need to do is punch the opponent's face with the other hand. *(Unless you have only one arm!)* In pain and shock, the opponent will automatically let go of your hand.

This follows the WingTsun principle: **"Refrain from fighting against the fully reinforced part of your opponent but attack his unprepared part"** (棄實 擊虛)

It is a pity that many martial artists tend to focus too much on complicated anti-clutching techniques in order to get out of the grip of an opponent. Consequently, they ignore the most efficient method of getting out of a strong grip, the one that actually does not need any brute force. If a combatant always has to depend on applying brute force against his opponent, then there would be no Martial **Arts,** just "beast fighting"!

112

Diagrams: 1 — 6:

The *Tut-sau* & Thrusting-punch sequence in the Siu-Nim-Tau set demonstrated by the late Great Grandmaster Yip Man in 1972. A few days later he passed away. Photos extracted from one of the two 8 mm movies treasured by Prof Leung Ting.

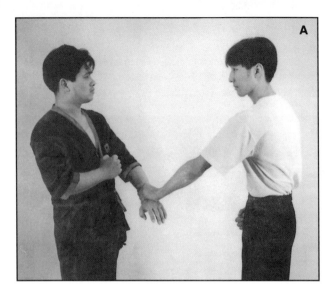

Diagram A – E

B (left) suddenly grabs **A**'s left wrist with his left hand. **A** ignores the grip but attacks **B**'s face with a right Thrusting-punch. **B** could never suspect that **A** would ignore his grip and attack him on the face without warning. Surprised and defenseless, **B** gets seriously hurt.

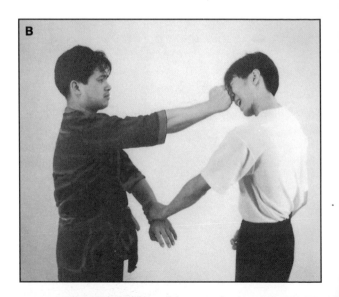

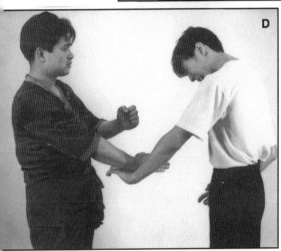

While **B** is in such pain that he cannot keep a firm grip on **A**'s wrist, **A** uses his right hand to chop **B** on the wrist-joint of the grappling hand, drawing back his left hand simultaneously. This is the *Tut-sau* technique from the Siu-Nim-Tau set.

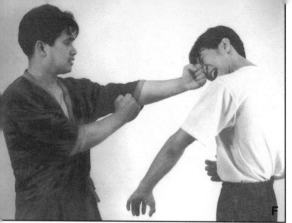

Diagram E – F

Now that **A** has both of his arms free, he launches a series of Thrusting-punches as a counterattack. This is the famous *"Lin Wan Chung Kuen"* or Chain-punches of the WingTsun system.

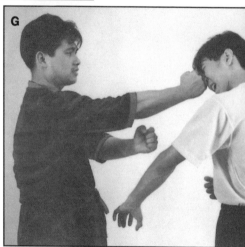

Demonstrators:

Sifu Lau Ka Sun

Assistant Instructor
Wong Wai Kin

ABOUT THE ESSENTIAL POINTS

SETTING UP THE "ONE-AND-A-HALF-PACE" STANCE

Since people come in different sizes, there is no "one-size-fits-all" stance. Instead we

have a formula to determine the correct width stance for each person. For instance, in the frontal stance, the feet should be separated by "one-&-a-half-pace". This is the best position to maintain stability, while remaining lively enough to move, change to another stance or launch a kick.

The correct method to get into this stance is as follows. First, lower the upper body by bending the knees *(Diagram A)*. Then, using the heels of your feet as pivots, turn both feet outward until they form almost a straight-line *(Diagram B)*. Finally, using the balls of your feet as pivots, turn the heels outwards until your feet form two sides of an equilateral triangle *(Diagram C)*.

ABOUT THE "CHARACTER TWO ADDUCTION STANCE"

The "Character 'Two' Adduction Stance", or "Adduction Stance" for short, is pronounced in Cantonese as, *"Yee-Gee-Kim-Yeung-Ma"* （二字拑羊馬）, which implies that the structure of the stance should be like both feet standing on the ground at a 60° angle with knees turned inward towards each other.

"Yee-Gee" means " Character 二" ("二" *means "TWO" in English*) in Chinese writing. This character consists of a short strip on top of a longer one. If a WingTsun practitioner were to place his heels on the ends of the longer strip and his toes on the ends of the shorter strip, his feet would make an angle similar to two sides of an equilateral triangle. The words *"Kim-Yeung"* should be translated as *"Riding a goat and gripping it with inward-rotated knees"*. This is how we apply force while practicing *Siu-Nim-Tau*.

When we turn our knees inward and hold them together strongly, we form a kind of interlocking force between our legs. Because of this strong force, even if an opponent suddenly attacked us with, for example, a sweep-kick, we would not be easily knocked down.

Right Diagram:

The late Great Grandmaster Yip Man demonstrating the "Character 'Two' Adduction Stance"

Above: A lack of interlocking force causes the lower limbs of the practitioner to relax and become more likely to collapse when being attacked by a sweeping kick.

Below: The interlocking power locks two knees together, making the lower legs act like a single unit, thus the center of gravity becomes very stable.

When practicing the Siu-Nim-Tau set, in addition to the points mentioned in page 14, there are several other mottoes that help the practitioner in the attainment of inner strength and correct movements.

Push the Head against the Sky & Stand Firmly on the Ground
(頂天立地)

When a WingTsun practitioner performs the Adduction Stance, his body should be fully erect, as if he is pushing upward with all his might in fear that the sky is about to fall. 'Stand Firmly on the Ground' means the practitioner presses downward with his feet, as if he fears the ground will shake from under him.

In this stance, he should not hang his head down with a loose neck. A practitioner who allows his body and neck to loosen appears to wither and have a broken neck. This is the worst possible posture and practitioner is cautioned not to adopt such a pose.

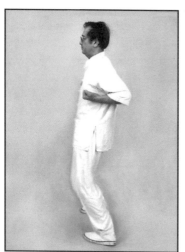

⇦ **Right Posture demonstrated by Grandmaster Leung Ting:** His head is up. His body 'from the shoulders to the knees' forms a straight line. His upper body does not lean back, nor does his chest push out.

Wrong posture: This man's head hangs down, his body sags, and his feet are slack as though he is about to fall. This is the worst possible posture. ⇨

𝕳ead up with 𝕳orizontal 𝖁ision（登頭平視）

Unlike WingTsun, other kungfu styles mainly use the 'front-stance'. Therefore, the head is commonly positioned forward, and in some styles (e.g. boxing) the fighters are deliberately trained to fight with their head bent downward in order to protect their throats.

In contrast, the WingTsun practitioner normally uses a 'rear stance' posture. This difference reflects WingTsun philosophy, which does not favor using brute force when fighting an opponent. The 'rear stance', makes it possible to achieve the purpose of deflecting forces exerted by the attacker. Therefore, our attacking stance takes the shape of a right angle triangle when viewed from the side.

The head is the most important part of the body. If one is hit on the head, one might be knocked unconscious and loose the ability to fight.

Therefore, we keep our head up, which is equivalent to placing our head at the furthest distance from our opponent. In this way, if a WT practitioner and another fighter both punch at each other's heads simultaneously, the other fighter must punch several inches further than the WingTsun practitioner, and the WingTsun practitioner has a better chance to avoid being hit

In a combat situation, if one does not remain focused on one's opponent, one's reactions will be sluggish when that opponent launches an attack. This lack of concentration and visual contact could also cause one's attacks to miss their mark. This is the reason that WingTsun encourages the mindset, "the eyes follow the hands".

Below: Bending the head forward (right) decreases the distance between one's head and one's opponent. By keeping one's head up (left), the distance between the attacking arm and one's head is increased.

Containable Chest and Elevated Back (涵胸拔背)

Due to ignorance about the ancient academic meaning of the first Chinese "涵" (pronounced as *"harm"*), which means *"containable, wide-ranging…"*, and because the pronunciation of this word is very close to another Chinese word "含" (pronounced as *"hum"*), which has the rather similar meaning *"swallowing, caving-in or containable"*, the true meaning of "涵胸" is often *misinterpreted* as *"Caving in of the chest"*.

In fact, the term **"<u>Containable Chest</u>"** means that one must relax the chest as much as possible, in order to feel the "containable chest cavity". This theory suggests that the chest should be like a half-inflated balloon. This state enables the chest cavity to absorb the force of an attack even when one is being brutally hit. Thus, even if one is injured, the injury will be slight. In contrast, if one tenses up his chest, not only is one unable to breathe freely, but also when one gets hit, the body cannot swallow-up much of the external power, and the injury inflicted will be severe.

Due to the misunderstanding of the first phrase of the motto, the second phrase (拔背), as a rule, is frequently misinterpreted as "protruding of the upper back" because people think that once if the chest is caving-in, "the back should be protruding" as well. This makes the practitioner look like he is a hunchback.

The second phrase actually means **"<u>Elevated Back</u>"** which means that one should stand with *"the back straight and elevated"*, like the standing of a lone peak.

Correct posture demonstrated by Prof Leung (left): Please note that he is totally relaxed yet his back is straight and upright. *(See also pg.123 side-view of the late GGMr Yip Man, who in his old age was still able to maintain this posture)*

Incorrect (right): His chest caves in and his back is in a "bow" shape. He'll have problems with the balance of his upper body and his breathing is bound to be shallow and inadequate.

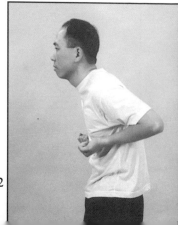

122

Straighten the Waist and 'Suck-In' the Abdomen (挺腰收腹)

"Straightening the Waist" and *"Sucking-in the Abdomen"* refers to making sure that neither one's buttocks nor one's tummy sticks out during practice. When the buttocks are pushed outward, it causes one's body to bend forward and consequently the head moves closer to the opponent. Bending forward will also cause one's balance to shift and could lead to falling forwards. When the tummy is allowed to stick out, the upper body will tend to lean backward causing a shift in balance, which could cause a practitioner to fall backwards. *"Sucking-in the abdomen"* also functions as a way to train the stomach muscles while practicing Siu-Nim-Tau.

Above: Side view of the Adduction Stance of the late Great Grandmaster Yip Man

Wrong posture A: Due to the tummy sticks outward, hence the upper body of the practitioner is leaning backward.

Wrong posture B: Since the practitioner's buttocks are pushed backward, causing his upper body to lean forward and his head is down.

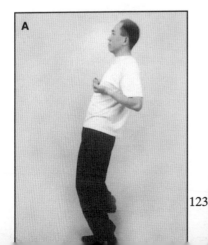

123

Incorrect (Above): Since the practitioner's buttocks are pushed backward, causing his upper body to lean forward, a slight pull by his opponent will cause him to fall forward.

Incorrect (Below): The practitioner sticks out his tummy, causing his upper body to lean backwards. If his opponent suddenly pushed him, he would fall backward easily.

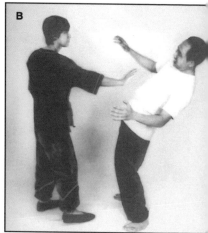

Correct (Above): The head is naturally positioned at the furthest distance from the opponent, thus minimizing the danger of being hit. If he is suddenly pulled, he is able to keep a right-angle triangular stance and darts into the stance of his opponent.

Correct (Below): With a correct frontal Adduction Stance, if his opponent suddenly pushes him, he can turn 45 degrees in either direction to deflect the power exerted by his opponent.

The Sinking Elbow & Drooping Shoulder (沈肘落膊)

As the above motto implies, when an arm-technique is being used, the elbow should be placed at the lowest possible position, and the shoulder should remain totally relaxed. If one practices Siu-Nim-Tau with unnatural breathing, stiff muscles and tensed-up shoulders, he will not be able to generate maximum power.

There is yet another theory behind the above motto. In a pre-fighting posture, a WingTsun practitioner places his hands at chest level in a fore and aft position. The arm closest to the body is not only used for attack, but is also used as a Protective-arm.

The elbow of the Protective-arm should be at waist level about one fist length away from the body. In this pose the hand can protect the chest and head, while the elbow can protect the waist and lower areas. Therefore, the elbow of the Protective-arm is similar to the bumper of a car. If the elbow is too high up, the protection for the waist is lost.

Above: Great Grandmaster Leung Ting demonstrating the *"Sinking Elbow and Drooping Shoulder"* posture.

Below: The elbow of the Protective-arm located about one-fist distance away from the waist in a pre-fighting posture is similar to the bumper of a car. Even if the WT practitioner is surprisingly attacked by his opponent to the waist position, the distance between the elbow and the waist still can "absorb" most of the attacking power before the fist touches the waist.

126

TWO OF THE MOST COMMON MISTAKES

Left Diagram:
This man tenses his muscles, causing his shoulders to rise. Therefore, his punches will be weak. Also, his elbow is too high, thus fails to protect his waist. His defense is easily penetrated.

Right Diagram:
This man is launching a punch with the elbow up. He would be easily counterattacked if his opponent hits upwards from underneath his punching arm.

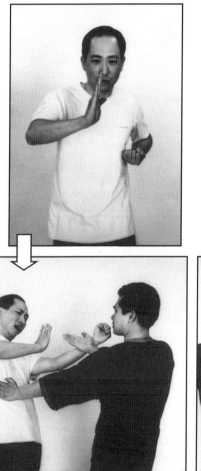

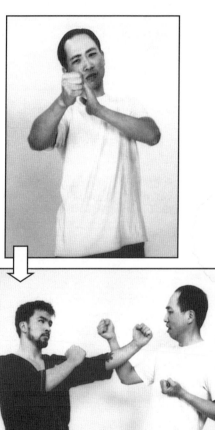

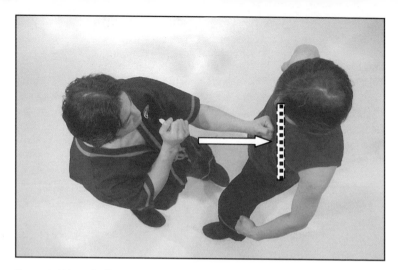

Correct (Above): The punch is launched along the centerline with the elbow sinking down. The punch resembles the action of a knife stabbing at perpendicularly towards the opponent, according to the motto of _"When launching a punch, keep the elbow in the middle"_.

Incorrect (Below): If the elbow is allowed to ride up, the hit will be made at an angle. When hitting something at a slant, the power of the strike is much weaker than when hitting something at a 90° angle.

The Centerline Theory

In WingTsun kungfu, the Centerline Theory divides a human body into two sections: the trunk and the four limbs. The trunk is the most important section. If any part of the trunk is cut off, one will die. However, if any, or even all, of the limbs are cut off, the trunk can still live. Therefore, the limbs function as protection for the trunk.

We have a unique course in WingTsun called "Footwork" or literately translated as **"Lower-level Kungfu"** （下盤功夫） which includes "lower-part fighting and defending techniques" such as kicks, stance-turning techniques and various step-techniques. It is actually the most important part of WingTsun, but was kept top secret traditionally in the older time.

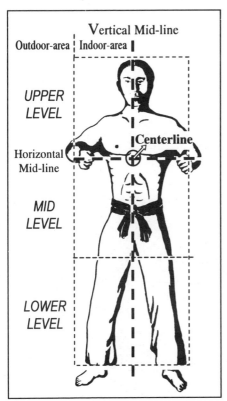

A WingTsun expert can use footwork not only for attacks, but also to protect his groin and all the weak points of his lower body. That is the reason there is no squatting movement to defend the lower limbs in WingTsun Kungfu because it is not necessary.

According to the WingTsun theory, the longer the "line of defense", the harder it is to protect. Since we do not have to protect our lower limbs, we can concentrate all our defending and attacking power within the short "line of defense" from the head to the groin only. This is the **"Close Application of Mid-level Attack"** (密集中門) fighting tactic.

It is also why the pre-fighting posture of a WingTsun practitioner is to place one hand in front of the other along the centerline, the "shortest straight-line", between him and his opponent. Once he occupies the shortest straight-line", his opponent has to take the longer line to attack. In this situation the WingTsun practitioner can attack or counterattack his opponent much more quickly than his opponent can attack him. This is the concept expressed in the motto: ***"While the others move along the back of the bow, we move along the bowstring"*** (人走弓背我走絃).

Right Diagram: A WT practitioner places one hand in front of the other along the Centerline. This enables either hand to take offensive or defensive action.

Below: Since both hands of the WingTsun practitioner (left) occupy the shortest straight line (Centerline) between him and his opponent, it doesn't matter if the opponent attacks the practitioner at upper level (left diagram) or at lower level (right diagram). The WT practitioner's punches can always land on the opponent's body earlier.

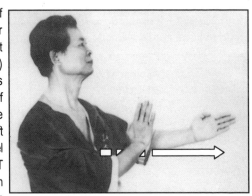